11 WAYS
— TO SERVE —
BUSY PARENTS IN A
BUSY WORLD

HEIDI HENSLEY

© 2014 Awana® Clubs International

Scripture quotations are from The Holy Bible, English Standard Version® (ESV®), copyright ©2001 by Crossway, a publishing ministry of Good News Publishers. Used by permission. All rights reserved.

TABLE OF CONTENTS

1. Know Your Parents And Families 8
2. Bring the Fun 12
3. Mentor And Be Mentored 16
4. Provide Realistic Discipleship Plans 20
5. Let Them Serve Together 24
6. Provide An Escape Route 28
7. Encourage Family Worship 32
8. Equip Parents For Spiritual Moments 36
9. Make Marriage A Priority 40
10. Celebrate 44
11. Involve Parents In The Kid Stuff 48

SERVING PARENTS

Breakfast and school, soccer, ballet, homework, and chores, oh my!

Does this sound familiar to anyone else? Families are busier than they have ever been, and there never seems to be enough time. When you pair this with the understanding that there really is no "typical family," it can be a little terrifying for the average church leader or parent.

So how do we successfully teach families to grow spiritually and minister to them? Whether you are a parent, grandparent, foster-parent, or ministry leader, we can benefit from getting on the same team for parenting!

1
KNOW YOUR PARENTS AND FAMILIES

KNOW YOUR
PARENTS AND FAMILIES

Gone are the days of assuming that every child has shown up to church with both parents and a sibling. If you are reading this as a ministry leader, then you know the family dynamic is no longer what it once was. Parents sometimes are not even necessarily the actual parents by definition. Grandparents raising children, single moms or dads, older siblings, aunts and uncles and adoptive parents are just a few parent models we now see these days.

With every one of these situations comes a different set of needs.

In order to serve these parents we need to know them. It's no coincidence that Jesus asked questions; did He really not know what blind Bartimaeus needed in Mark 10:46-52?

Of course not, but Jesus was a communicator. He showed interest in people's lives, and was genuinely interested in their physical and spiritual needs. As leaders, this can be as simple as being visible and available for conversation to learn more about the parents you serve.

# 2 BRING THE FUN

BRING THE FUN

We need to remember that rest and work are necessary, but often times we forget that fun is necessary also.

Parents are busy, families as a whole are busy, and it is so easy to get caught up in a routine or schedule and not have fun together. Some of us are natural silly-hearts, and others need to be taught or just given the opportunity.

I love the way Ecclesiastes 8:15 states: *And I commend joy, for man has nothing better under the sun but to eat and drink and be joyful, for this will go with him in his toil through the days of his life that God has given him under the sun.*

Opportunities to set aside work and laugh are needed. Something as simple as a game night or park games are often a welcome gift for families. A simple reminder to laugh during your week, will often allow an exhale from the busyness in life and create some great family memories in the process.

3
MENTOR
AND BE MENTORED

MENTOR AND BE MENTORED

It can be terrifying to raise a child. While many parents will seek mentorship for career or finances, there seems to be an expectation that when it comes to parenting, we should just know how.

If you are raising a child, you know this thought process isn't true. Proverbs 27:17 reminds us: *iron sharpens iron, and one man sharpens another.*

The King James Version says ... *sharpeneth the countenance of his friend*.... I love that. I know that none of us has all the answers, so in the midst of everything happening in our world, finding a person to keep us sharp as parents, to voice our concerns, and pray with is a blessing indeed.

Something as simple as encouraging parents to connect or even exchange emails as prayer partners can cultivate these mentoring relationships.

No matter how busy a parent is, knowing that others are experiencing some of the same trials and victories is encouraging and gives us strength.

4
PROVIDE REALISTIC DISCIPLESHIP PLANS

PROVIDE REALISTIC
DISCIPLESHIP PLANS

A few years back, I found a book with a 12-month family discipleship plan. After a stressful day at work, learning that a science project was due the next day, and having no idea what to make for dinner, I was determined to start this plan. After all, a few moments as a family around the Word would be amazing, right? We sat down at dinner table and I opened Lesson 1. For this lesson, I discovered that I needed six containers of play dough, a toothpick, a button, and a marble. Not cool! We closed the book, read a Psalm, and called it a night!

After that experience, I wondered just how many times I had asked the families in our church to do just the same type of thing.

And these words that I command you today shall be on your heart. You shall teach them diligently to your children, and shall talk of them when you sit in your house, and when you walk by the way, and when you lie down, and when you rise. You shall bind them as a sign on your hand, and they shall be as frontlets between your eyes. You shall write them on the doorposts of your house and on your gates. (Deut. 6:6-9)

By teaching parents to identify life's teachable moments, family discipleship becomes easy. Things like asking questions in the car during the week, or verses that are simply read and discussed bring topics to parents in the midst of what is happening rather than trying to squeeze in yet another thing or activity.

Consider creating a monthly focus that will allow parents to tailor it to their own "doorposts" as well as bring community between the other families in your church. This also allows parents with no church background to gain biblical knowledge along with their kids, and as you learn more about your parents this can help you design the content you hand out.

5

LET THEM SERVE TOGETHER

LET THEM SERVE TOGETHER

Kids know what is important to their parents. They see our every move and reaction at home, but what about outside the home? Your child may know you went on a mission trip, or served at a shelter, but do they know why? Often times kids catch fire for what their parents are passionate about; this is why you see generations of physicians or pastors. I personally love to see the generations of lay people, because often you will see a family who served together and had the kids involved from a very young age.

While I always encourage parents to share their testimony of salvation with their children, it's awesome when their children get to be an eyewitness and even a counterpart in their parent's Christian walk. As parents, taking the initiative to serve in ways that can involve your children will show them your love and passion for serving Christ and loving others. In Nehemiah 3, when you read about the rebuilding of the wall of Jerusalem, there is a listing of all the people who were credited for building parts of the wall. The fascinating part of this story is how many family members who worked together to complete the task. This was a moment of family ministry in Scripture!

Opportunities for families to serve together are so important, because they offer moments where parents are able to invest in their children spiritually. Whether you offer a foreign mission trip for families, a day long serving opportunity, or ways to serve in your church like parents and kids ushering, these age-appropriate moments will allow parents and kids to catch a vision for serving Christ together.

6
PROVIDE AN ESCAPE ROUTE

PROVIDE AN ESCAPE ROUTE

Parents (and kids) can have so much happening around us and miss each other completely! Adding to the busyness, parents and kids have smartphones, tablets, and TVs pulling what energy we have left.

An excellent way to serve busy parents is to provide an escape route. For our church this looked like a snow retreat, a weekend of technology-free fun for the families. We escaped, played games, threw snowballs, and separated into family units and talked about things like prayer and peer pressure. Discussions were long enough to open doors and short enough to be comfortable for tweens. There were some parents who told us that this was the first time their kids had opened up on certain topics, and a single mom who finally learned of some of her child's fears.

Over and over we see Jesus escape the noise to pray or be with God, Luke 6:12 tells us He went to a mountain and prayed all night, this is an example we can take and use as individuals and families. Jesus could have prayed where He was, but there is value in the quiet and time of removing yourself from the world to refocus on God. Kids obviously can't just escape, so as leaders and parents we need to provide this route for them.

ENCOURAGE FAMILY WORSHIP 7

ENCOURAGE FAMILY WORSHIP

Just like serving together, worshiping together is so important. Gone are the days of the family hitting the church doors and splitting in different directions for the entire day. Most families spend much of the week apart due to their busy lives and they want togetherness for worship time.

There will always be a need for age appropriate learning, and class or small group time, but when a child is old enough to experience corporate worship with the family unit, it is beneficial. This model or format can look very different: some churches have a family room where the service is televised and others welcome kids into the sanctuary for every service.

Hebrews 10:24-25 says: *And let us consider how to stir up one another to love and good works, not neglecting to meet together, as is the habit of some, but encouraging one another, and all the more as you see the Day drawing near.*

This Scripture has no age marker, and all too often kids are not introduced to corporate worship until adulthood. By providing ways families can worship together, parents are equipped to teach their children why worship is important. This also allows multi-generational interaction; kids will get to learn from some of the older saints and be an active part of the body.

8

EQUIP PARENTS FOR SPIRITUAL MOMENTS

EQUIP PARENTS
FOR SPIRITUAL MOMENTS

I love asking kids to tell me about their salvation experience, especially when their story includes a bedtime prayer with Mom or Dad. While most parents are comfortable praying with their children, there are more and more young parents entering the church for their kids' sake who have no faith background at all. By equipping parents for spiritual moments, we can also minister to them!

The easiest and first step is to have parents share their testimony with their children. Kids love a good story – especially one that involves their Mom or Dad. Whether parents share a "coming to faith" story or just what God is teaching them now, the power of testimony can be a catalytic moment in the life of a child.

Kids' ears perk up when parents are being transparent about their faith journey. Sharing how God is working in their lives shows kids that their parents are walking the same journey they are.

Parents can be taught the ABCs (ask, believe, confess) of salvation and encouraged to pray regularly with their children. A simple bookmark with Scripture reminders can be a starting point.

9 MAKE MARRIAGE A PRIORITY

MAKE MARRIAGE A PRIORITY

The foundation of a healthy family is a healthy marriage. That foundation should be firm, solid, and reliable. Hebrews 13:4 is just one of several verses about marriage. It begins by saying, *Let marriage be held in honor among all … We are called to love and honor.*

Often however, the first relationship to suffer – even in the godliest family – is the marriage relationship. Without care and attention, that foundation can begin to crack. Parents get busy. Left unchecked, that busyness easily undermines the foundation that they hope to build for their families.

Busy parents sometimes simply need to be reminded to honor and nurture their marriage relationship. Reminding parents to nurture their marriage can be a great opportunity to lead them by speaking to the relationship that they are most likely to neglect.

They also need to have fun together. Serving busy parents can look as simple as providing a movie night at church for the kids, while parents enjoy time together. By offering reminders, date nights or marriage classes for your church families, you can serve parents well and make marriage a priority.

CELEBRATE

Pausing to celebrate offers parents a time to reflect and rejoice in parenthood.

Whether looking at one of the many festivals (1 Corinthians 5:8), or celebrating a son returning home in Luke 15:23-24, celebration is throughout Scripture for a variety of reasons. Busy is busy, but usually somewhere along the line kids' lives are marked by achievements: soccer trophies, a mom's newly earned degree, a baby dedication, and baptism. These are all reasons to celebrate. By celebrating these events we become a stronger family community, invested in the lives of others and celebrating for the glory of God.

Celebration speaks directly into a child's spiritual formation and confidence: calling out identity and bringing spiritual gifts, personality, and skills forward. It's as if the faith community joins together and says, "Yes – you did it!" "Well done!" "Look at what God is doing in your life!"

If done well, celebration points to the reality that God is at work in a child's life. Done consistently over time, a child begins to feel that she is valued and that she has a role to play in God's story. Providing opportunities for parents to celebrate with their kids is a tangible way to serve them as they lead their children.

11
INVOLVE PARENTS
IN THE KID STUFF

INVOLVE PARENTS IN THE KID STUFF

Our last way to minister to busy parents is to simply keep them informed, invite them in, and open the doors for them to see what their child is learning about Christ.

Sometimes, we think that if we just handle something for a parent or child we are helping. The intention is to lighten their load, right? Even the busiest of parents are captivated by their children. They love to see them learning and growing, and to be involved.

Most churches have amazing leaders and teachers, but do your parents know what their kids are learning? Have they seen the classroom prayer wall, or the coat of many colors made from four different kinds of beans by their child?

By involving parents in children's ministry activities, you're giving them the opportunity to see Jesus from their child's perspective.

You never know, you may actually be sharing the gospel with a parent too.

HEIDI HENSLEY

Heidi Hensley is the Director of Children and Family Ministries at Quail Lakes Baptist Church in Stockton, California, where she has been serving since 2005. With 19 years of experience, Heidi is passionate about creating an atmosphere that allows kids to own their faith and equips parents to be their biggest support.

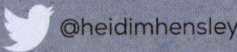 @heidimhensley 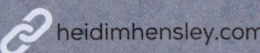 heidimhensley.com